Growing Up Curly

Dedicated To My Nieces

Genesis, Emery, and June

Growing Up Curly

PAGE:

1. **What Is Your Name?**
2. **Argentina**
3. **Bolivia**
4. **Chile**
5. **Colombia**
6. **Costa Rica**
7. **Cuba**
8. **Dominican Republic**
9. **Ecuador**
10. **Help Emery Find Her Comb!**
11. **El Salvador**
12. **Guatemala**
13. **Honduras**
14. **Mexico**
15. **Nicaragua**
16. **Panama**
17. **Paraguay**
18. **Peru**
19. **Puerto Rico**
20. **Help Connect The Items!**
21. **Uruguay**
22. **Venezuela**

Hi My Name Is
_____

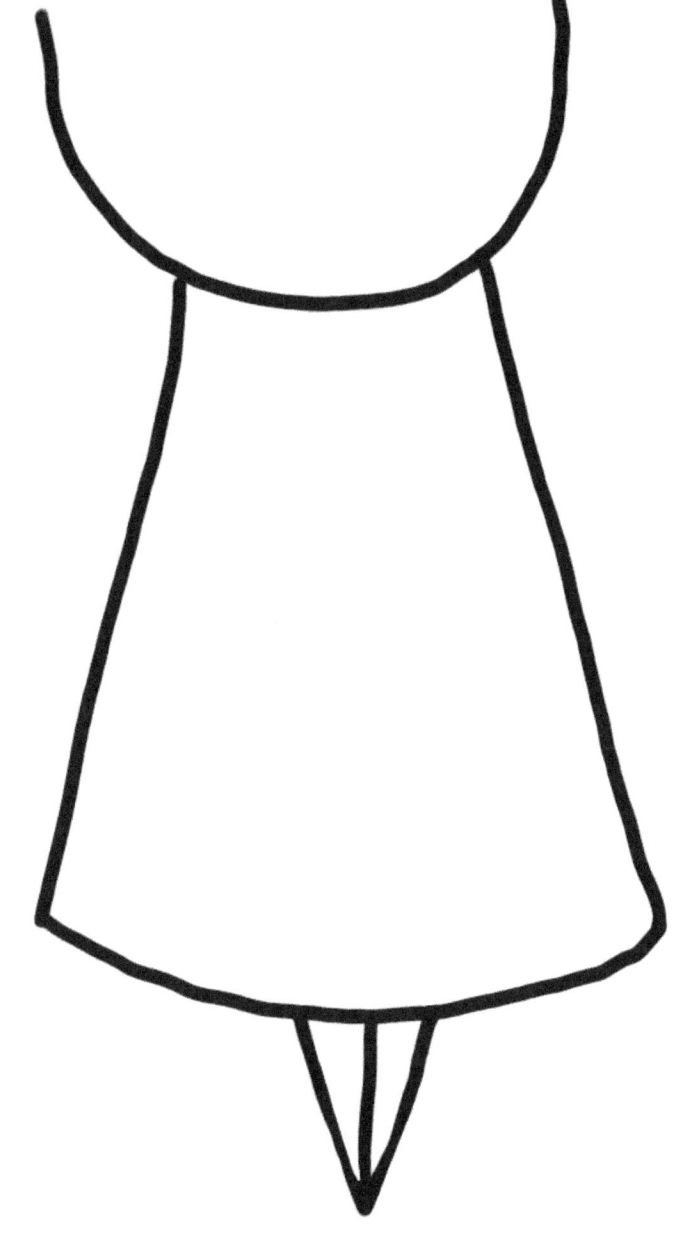

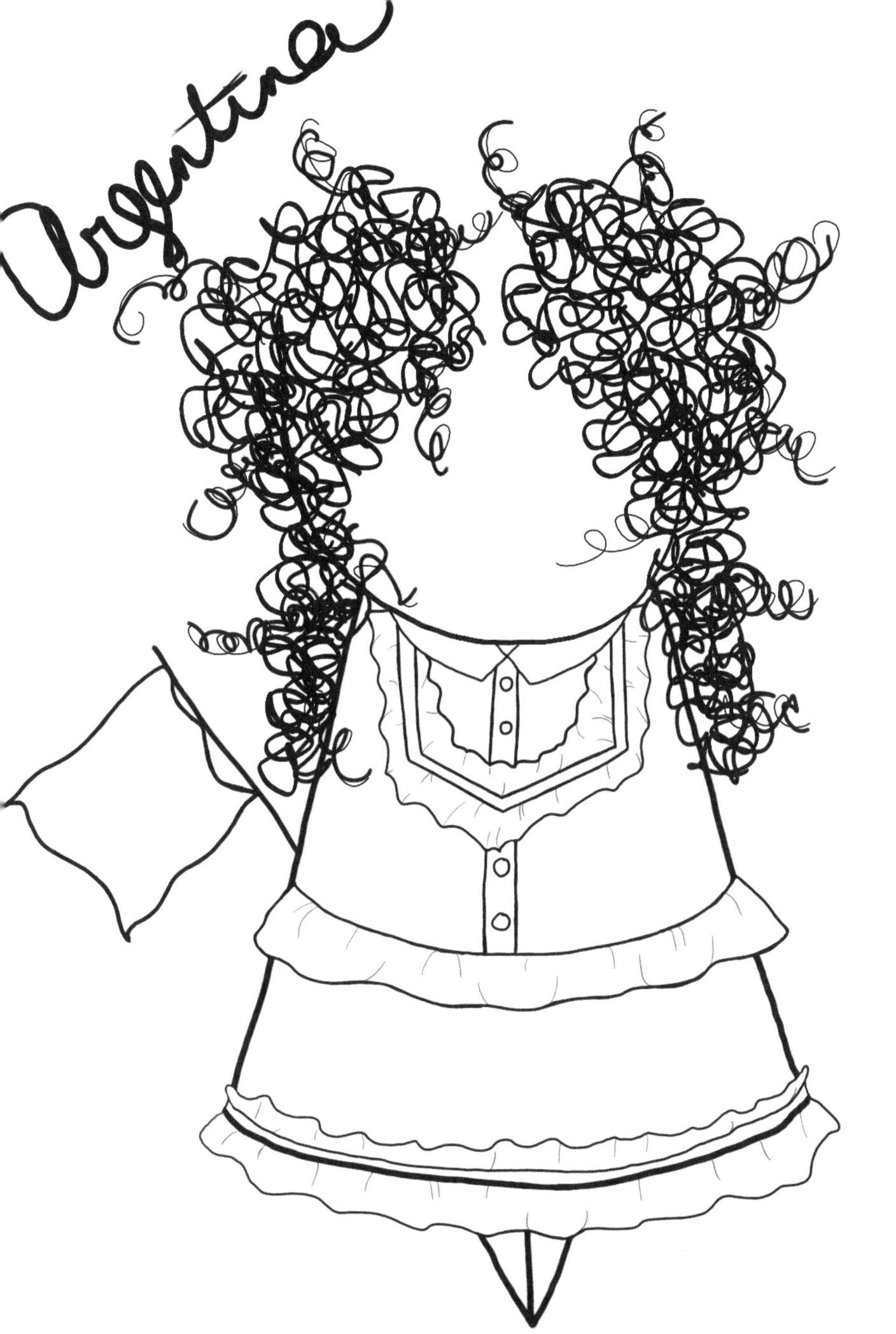

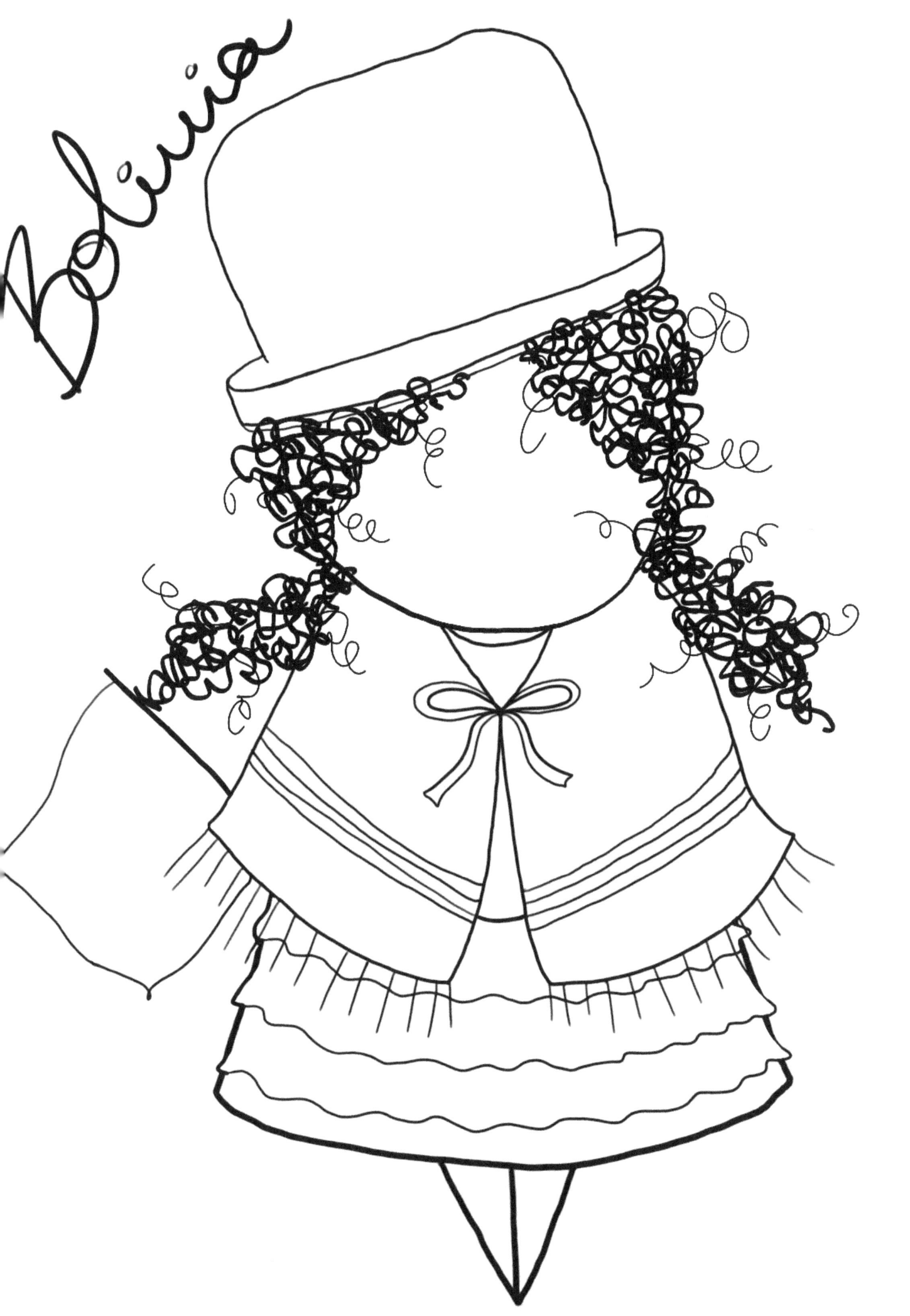

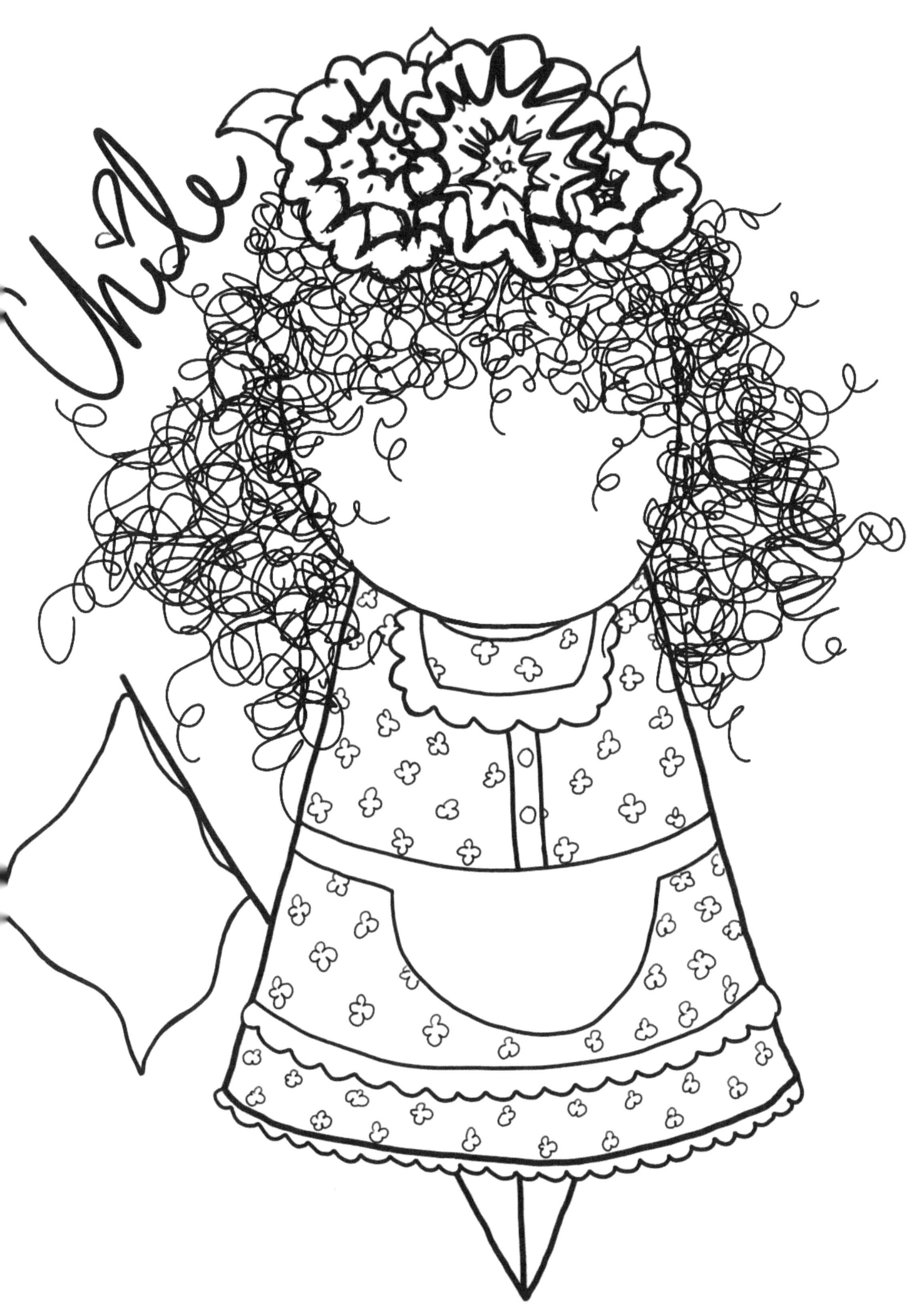

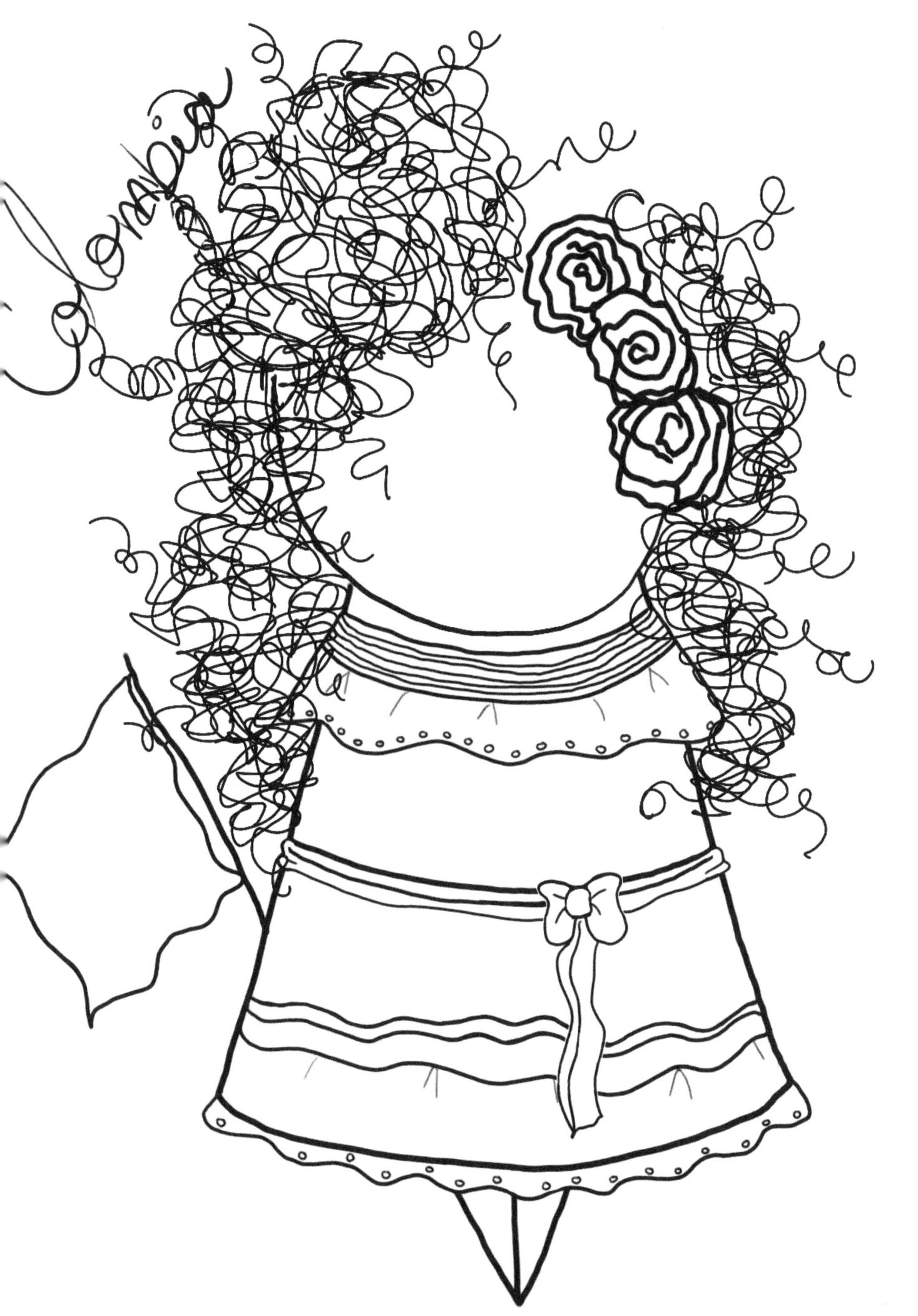

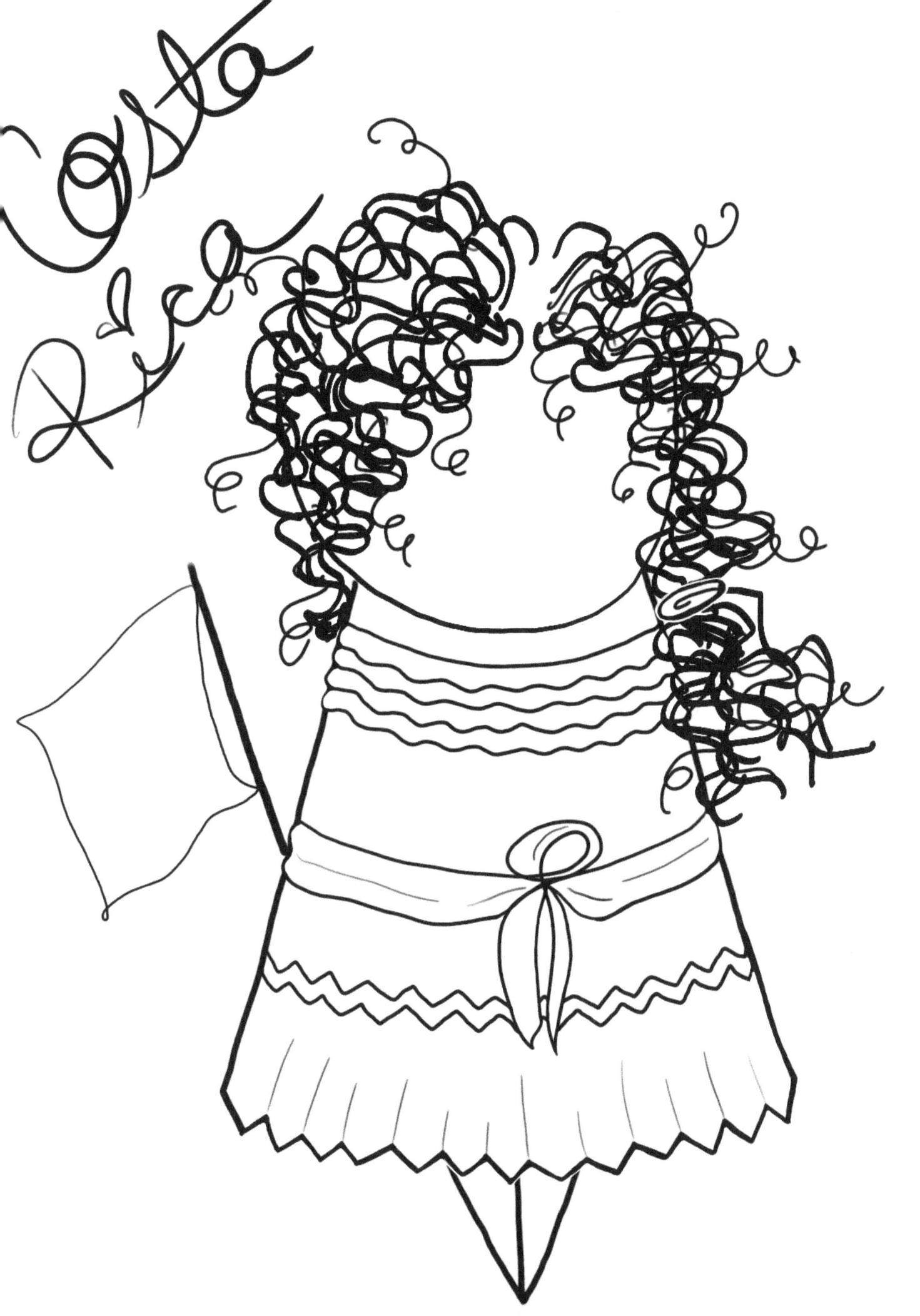

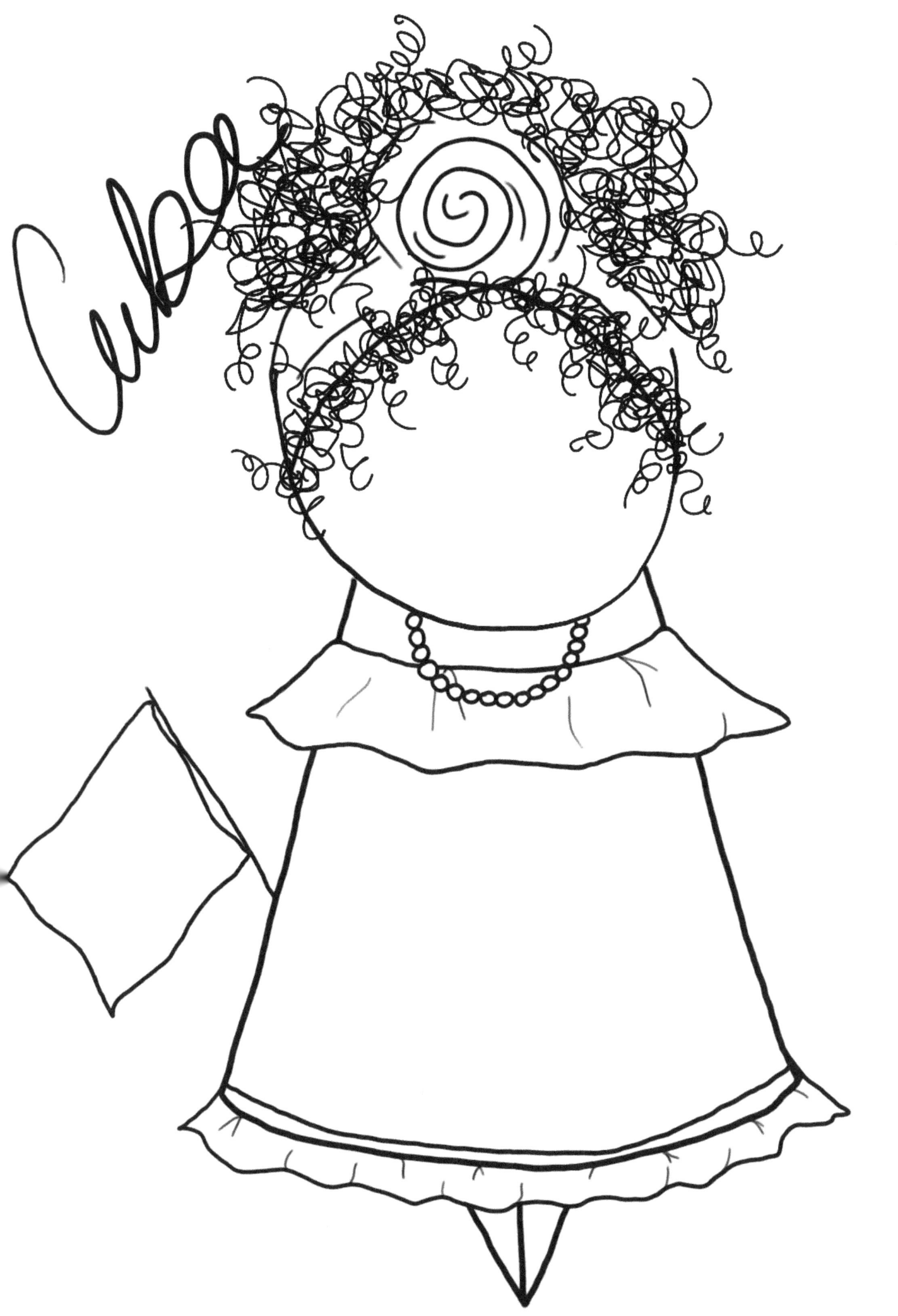

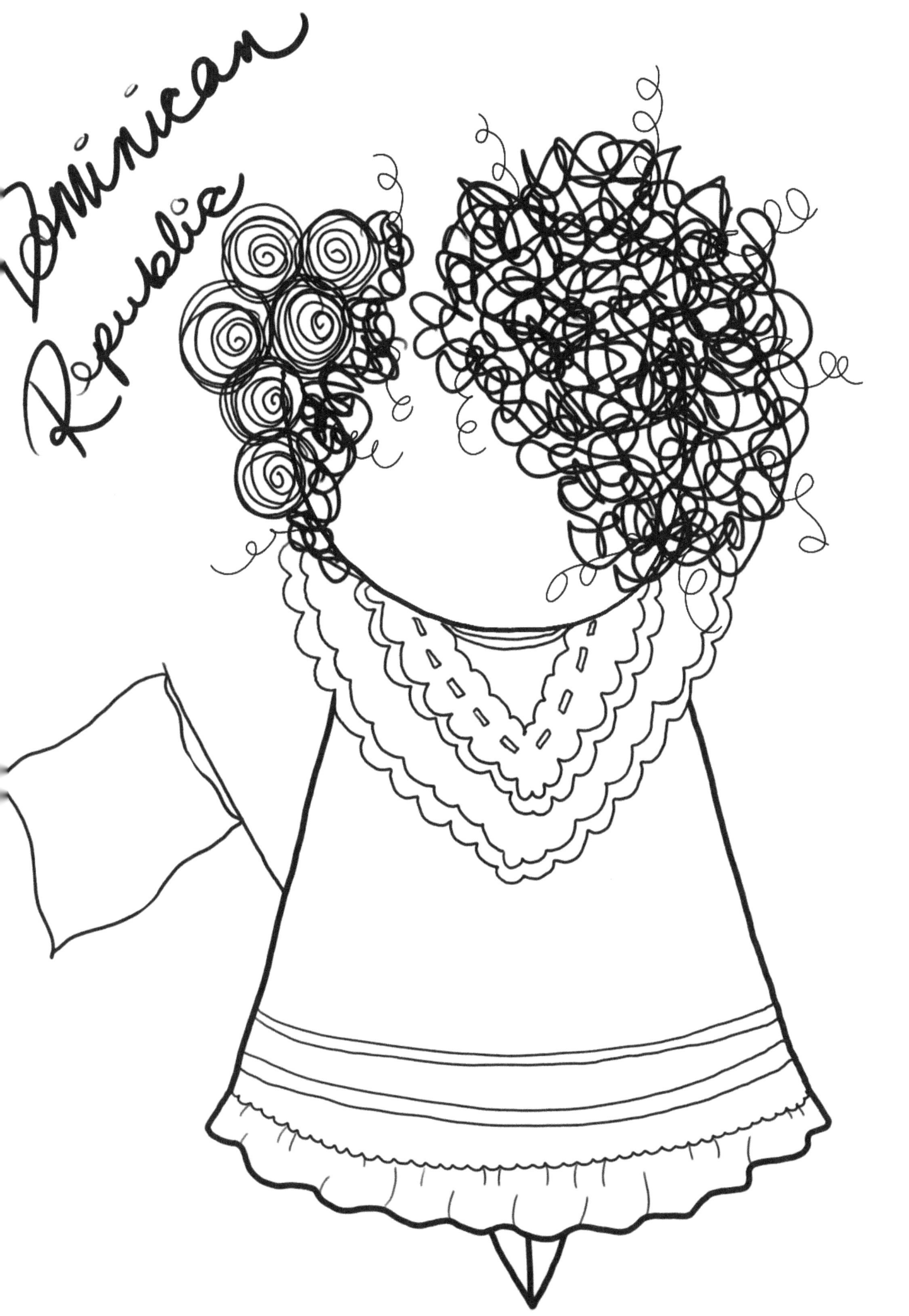

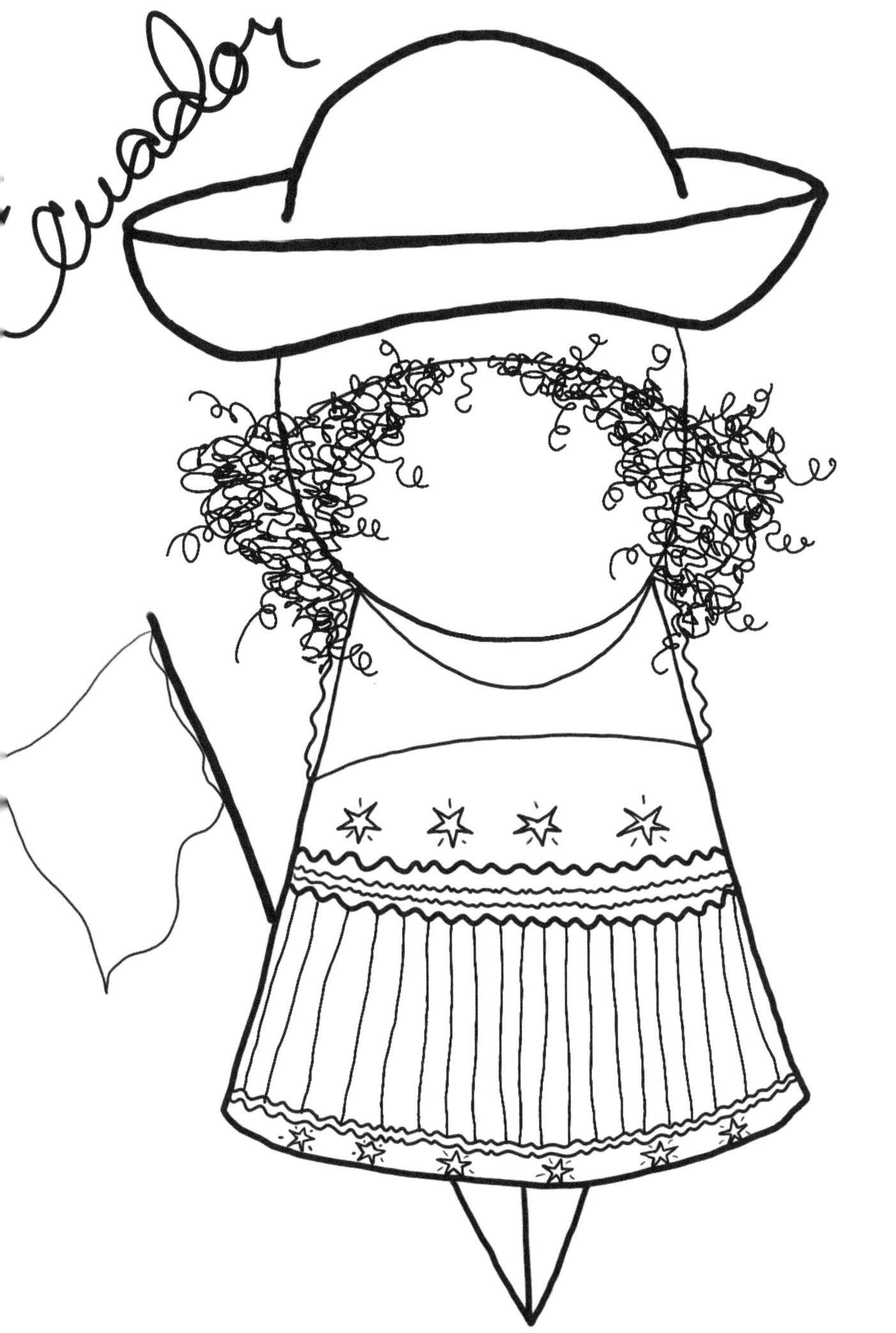

Find Emery's Comb

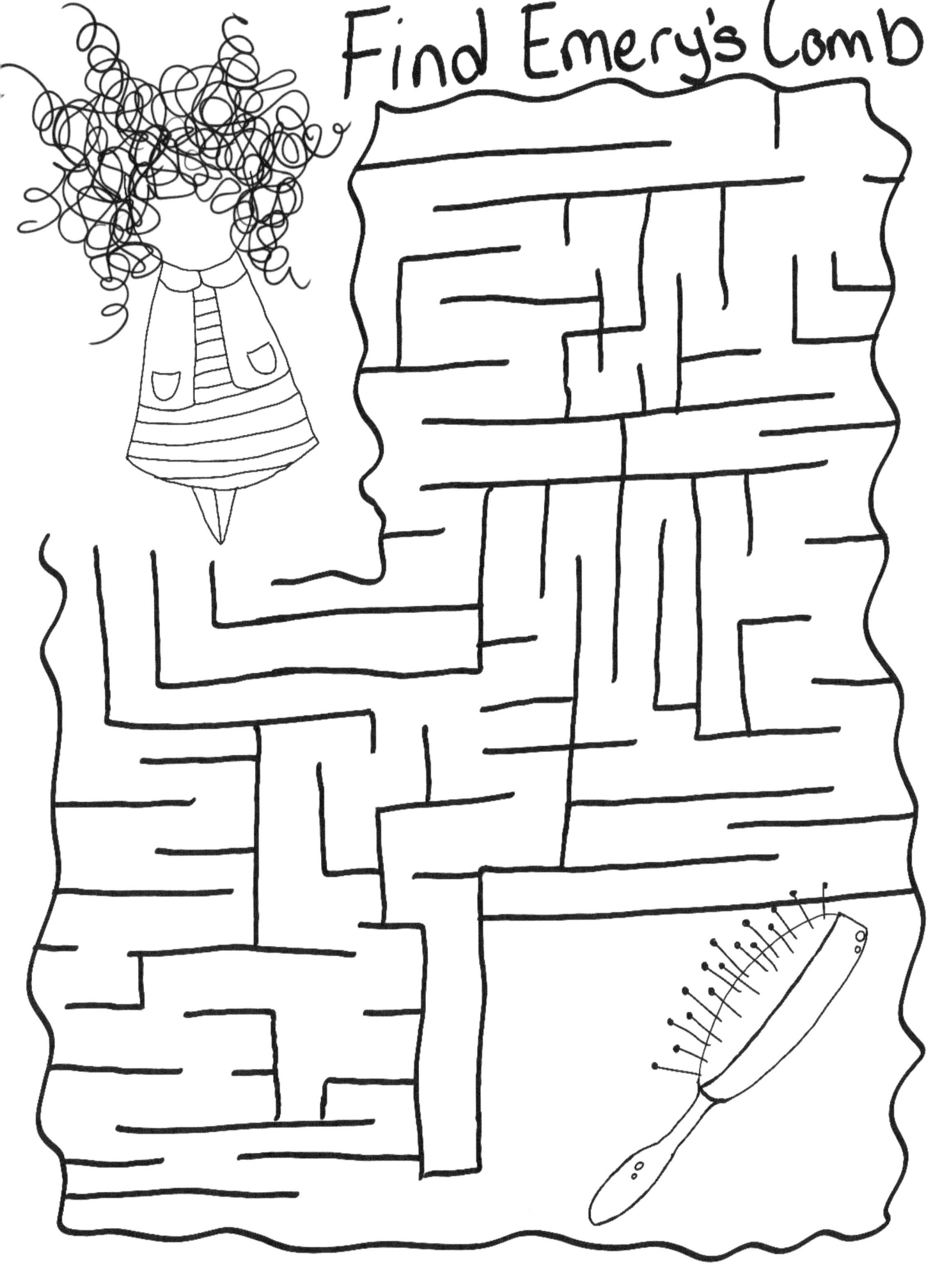

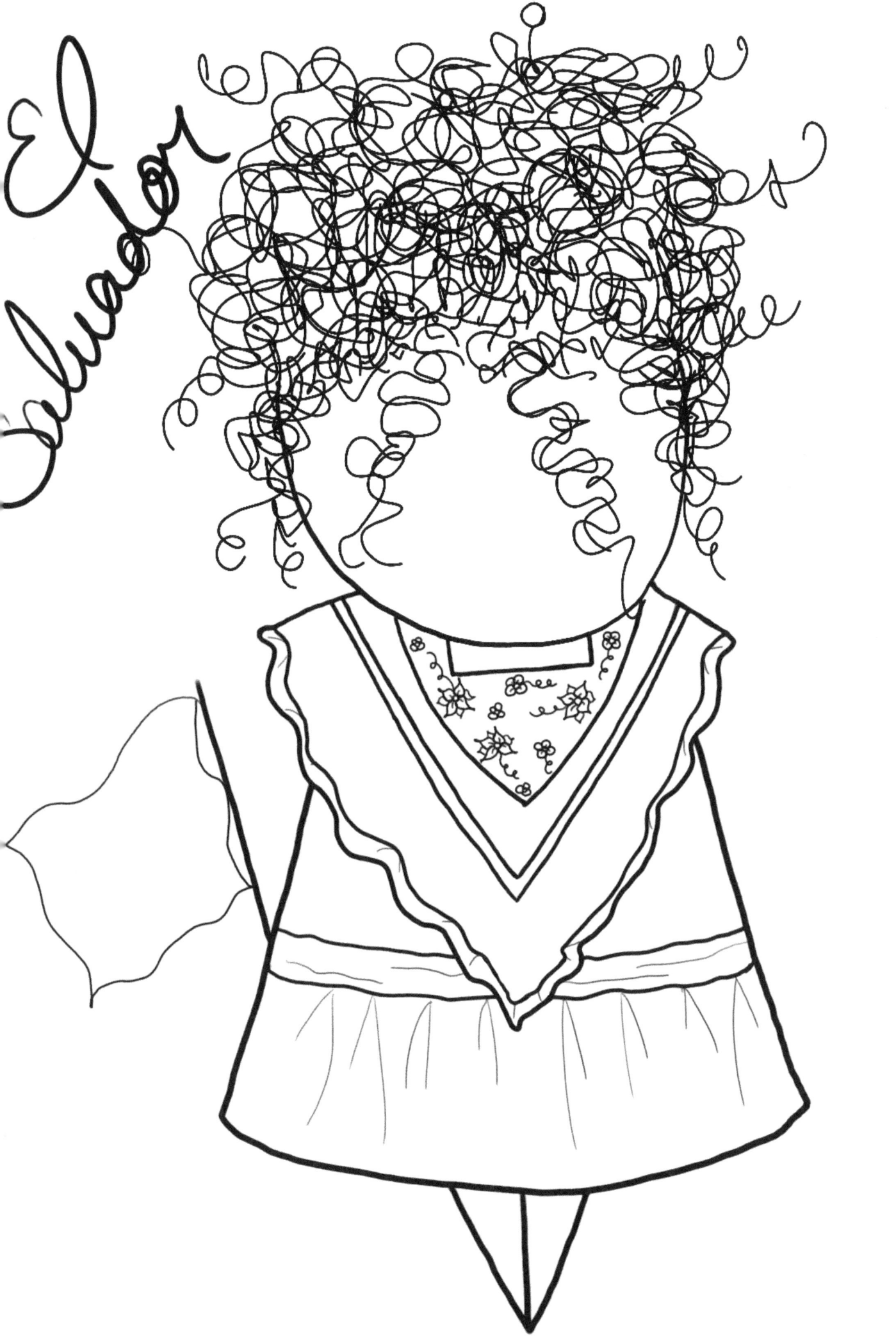

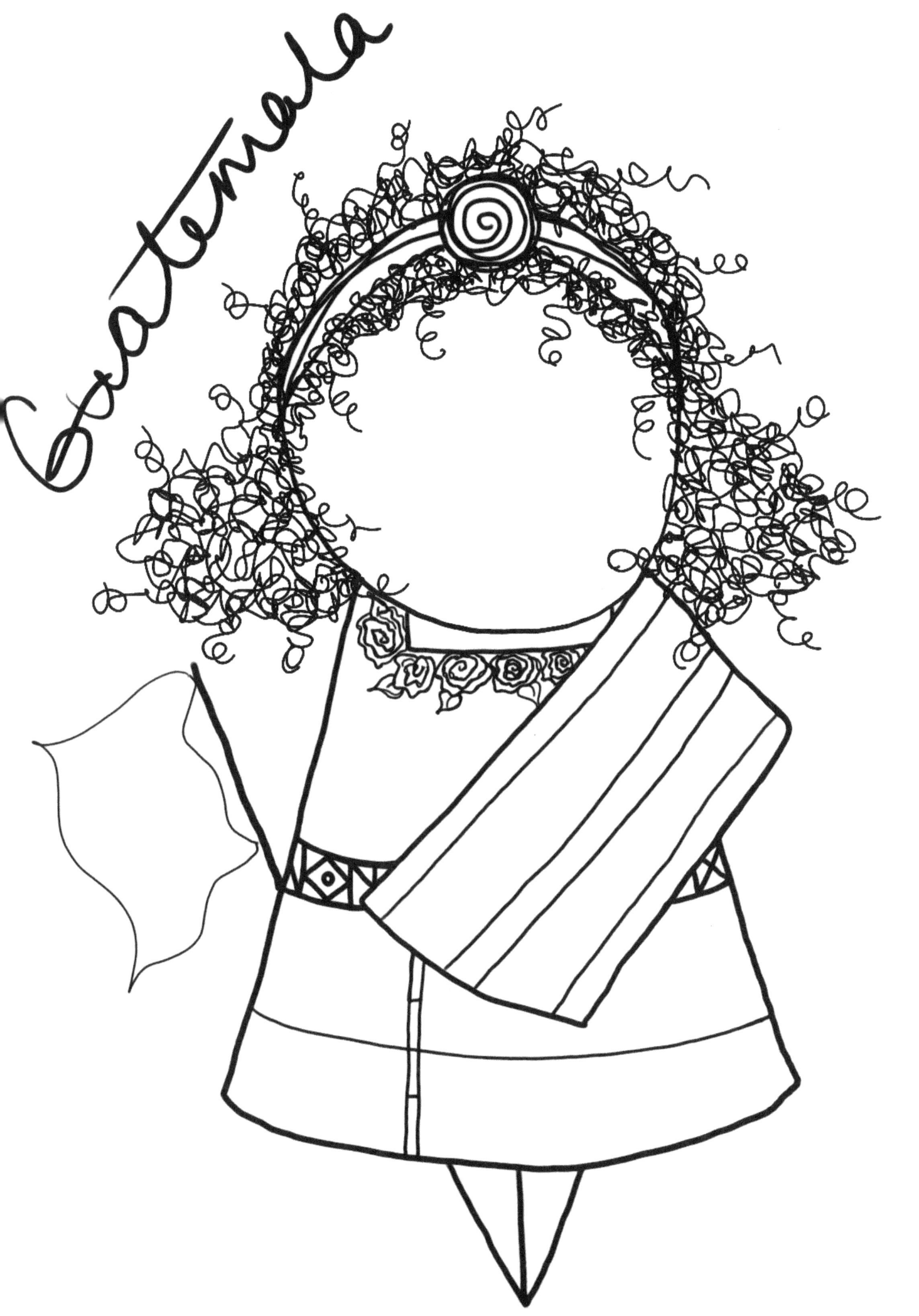

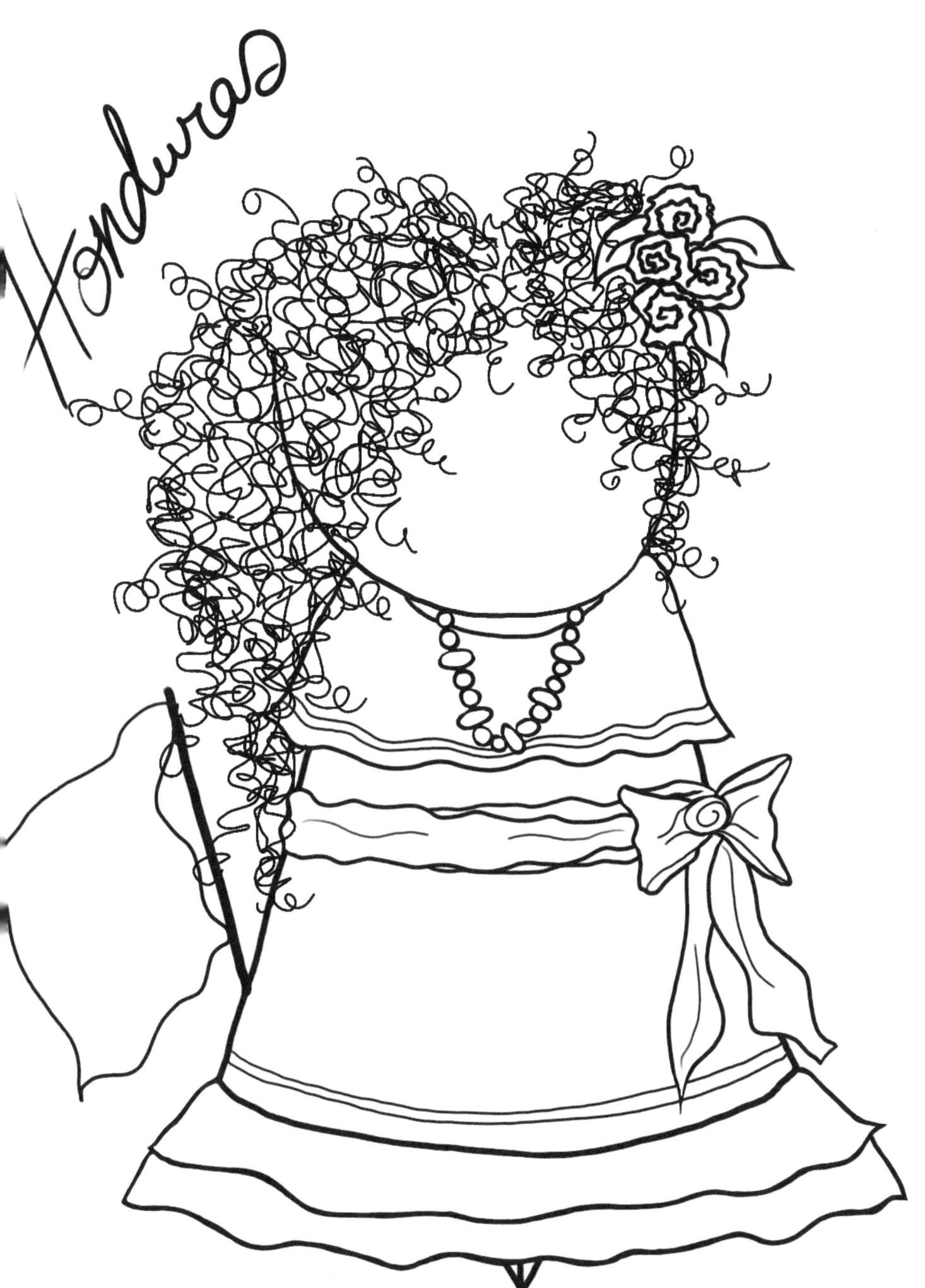

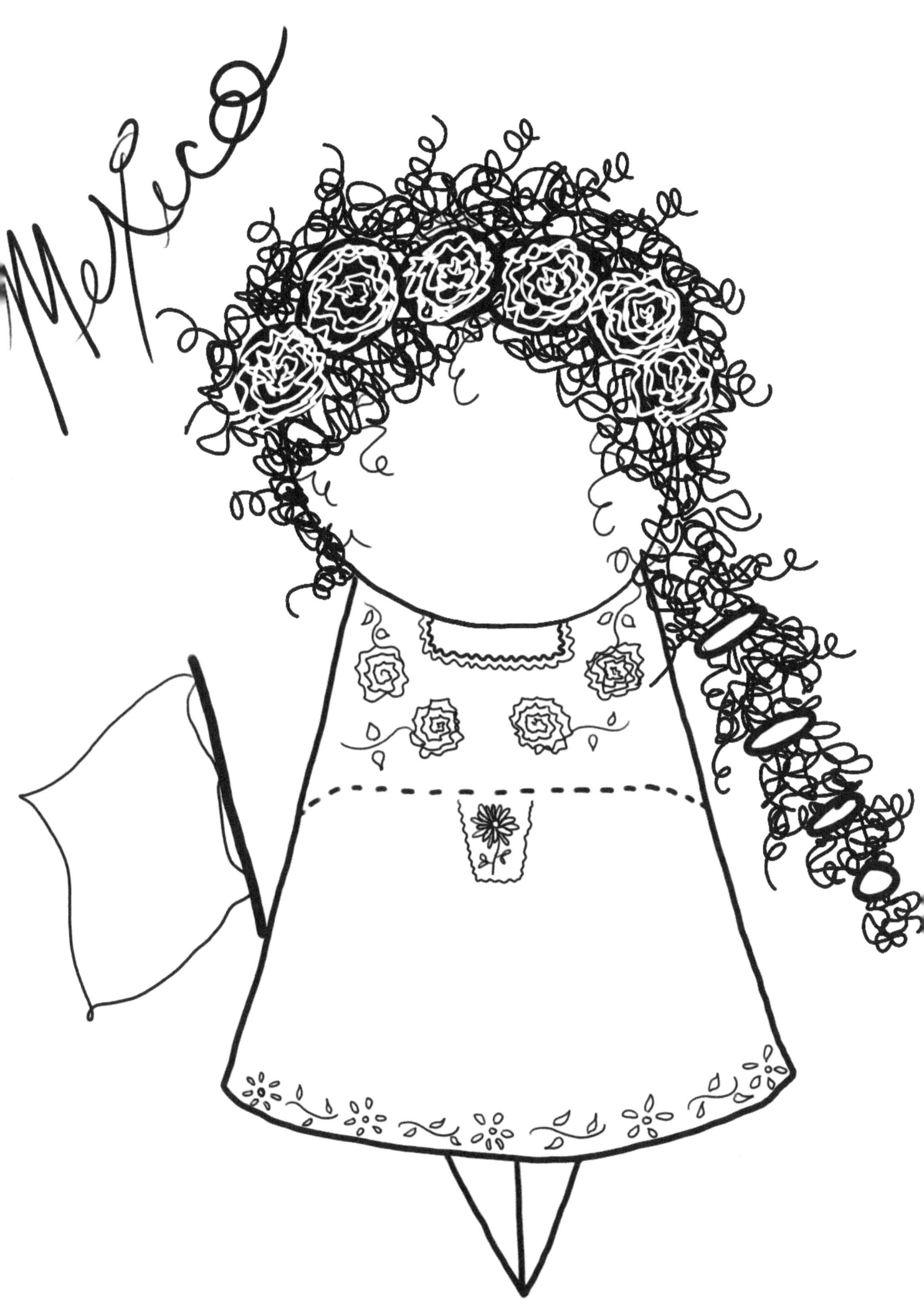

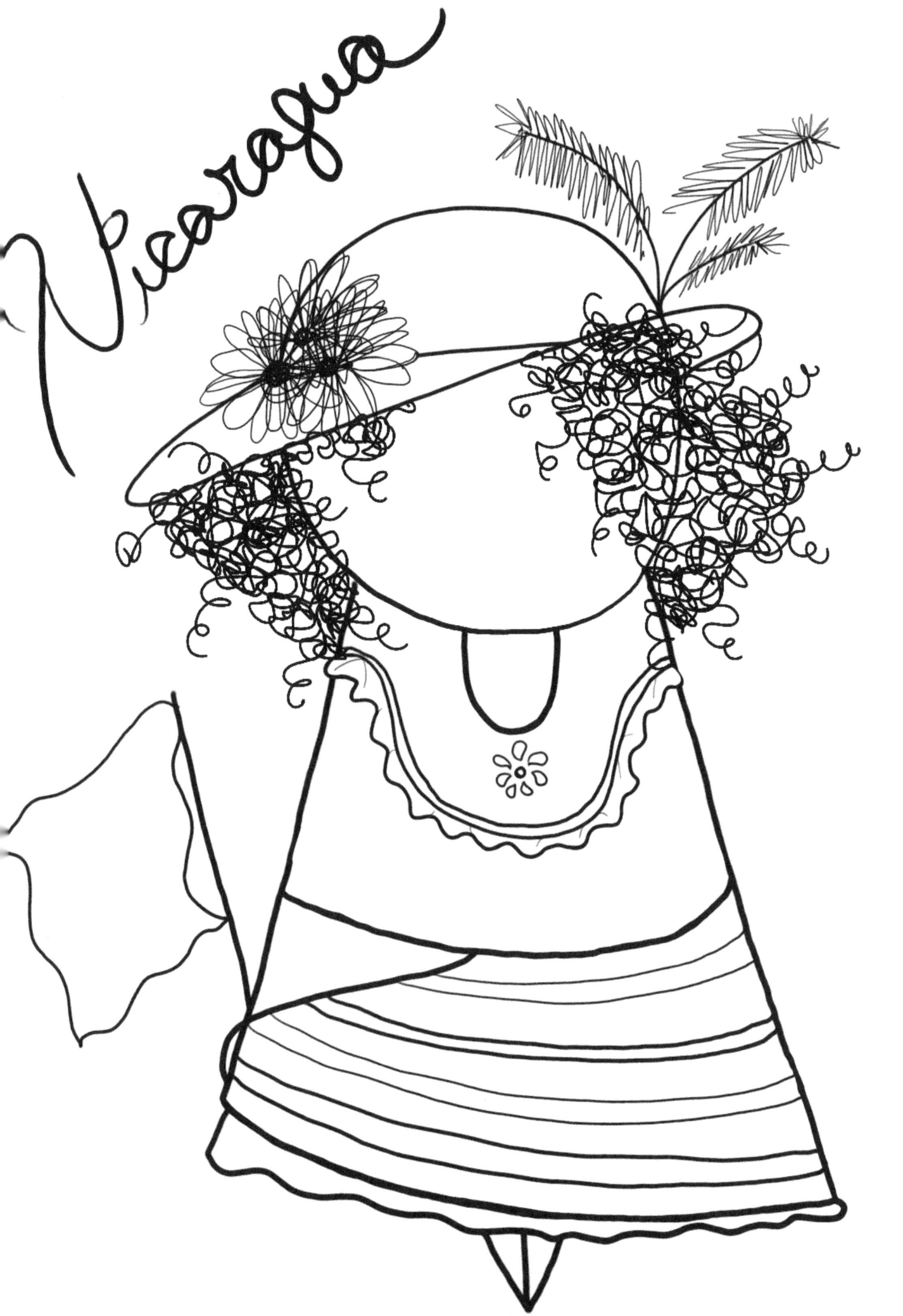

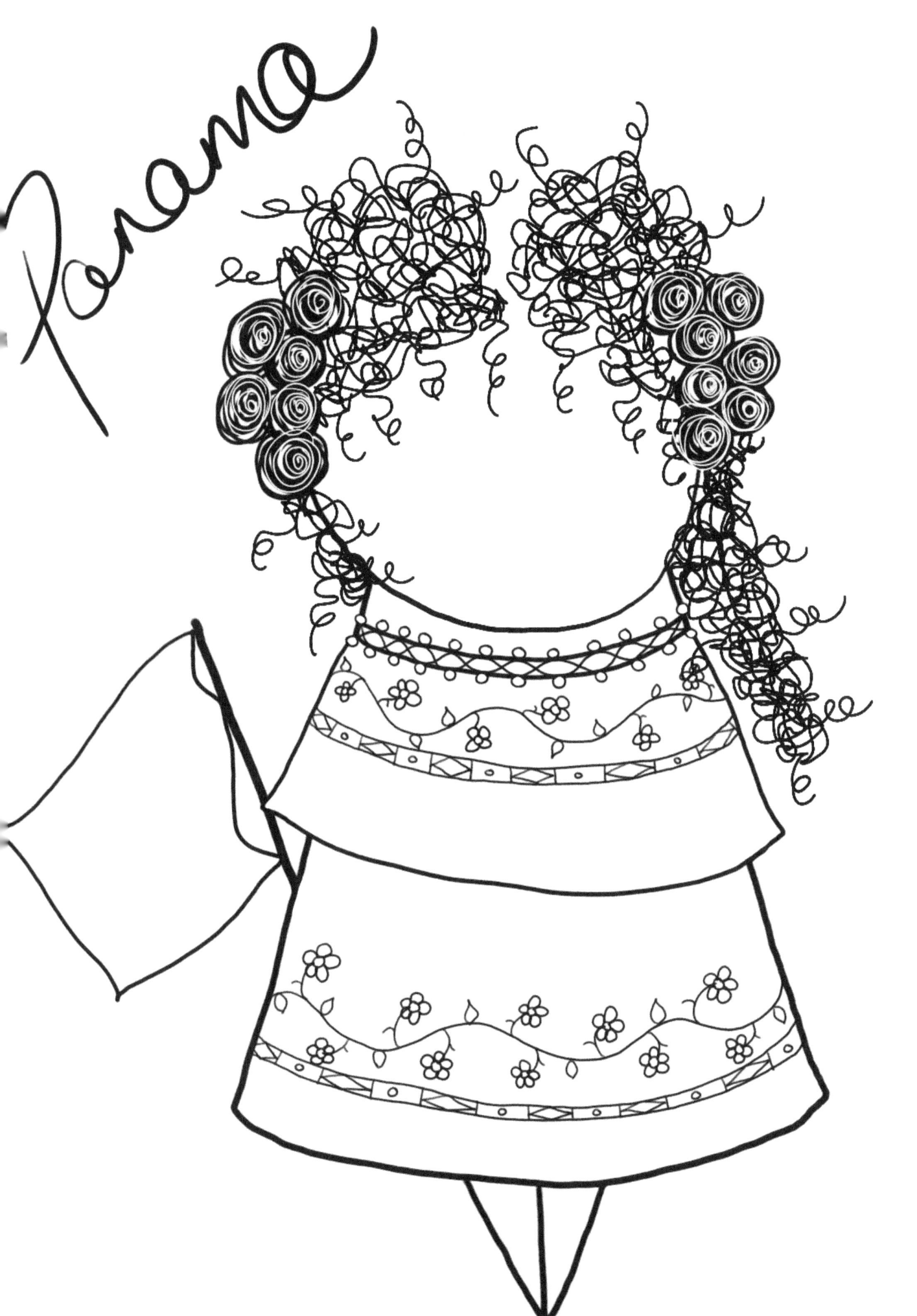

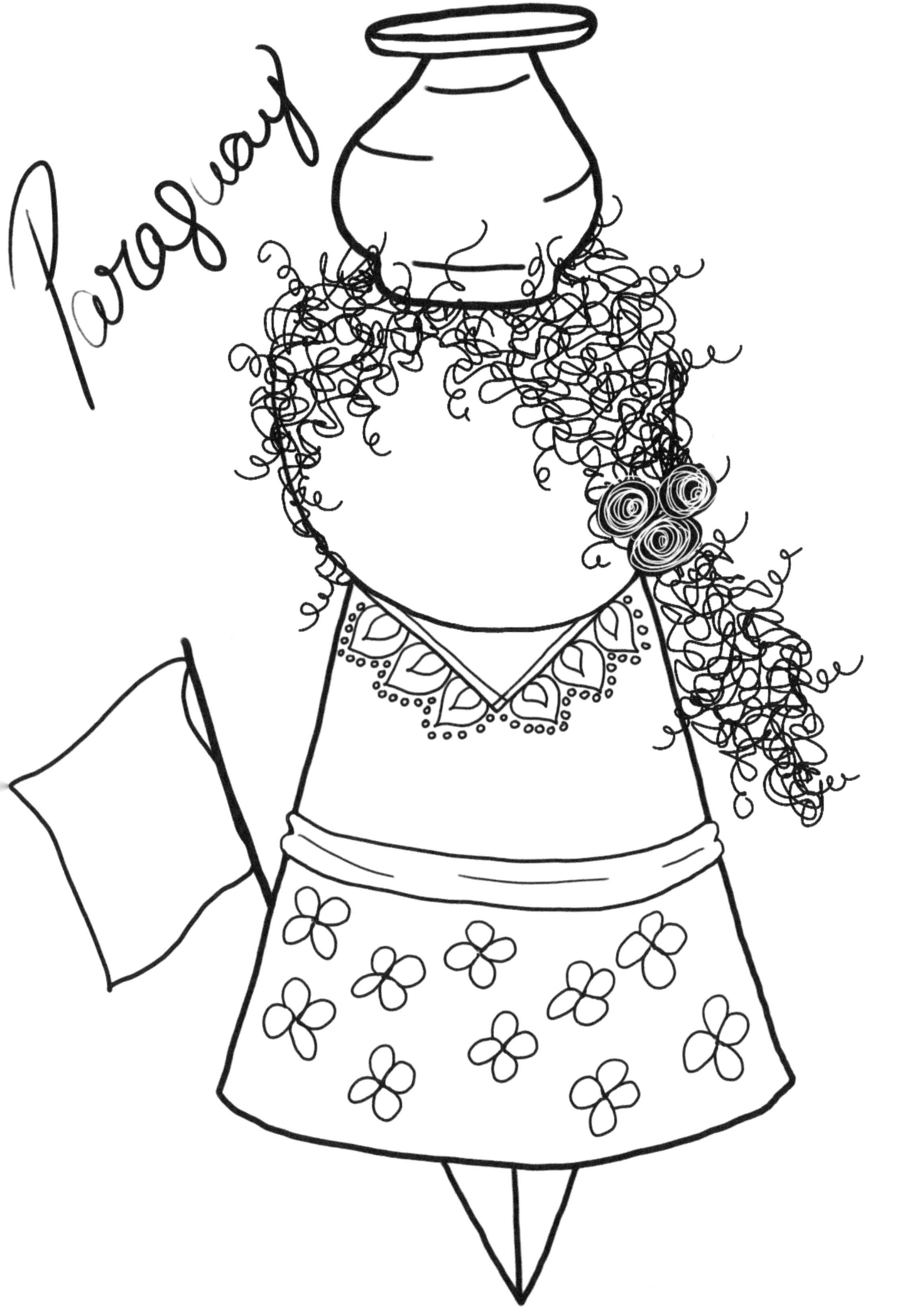

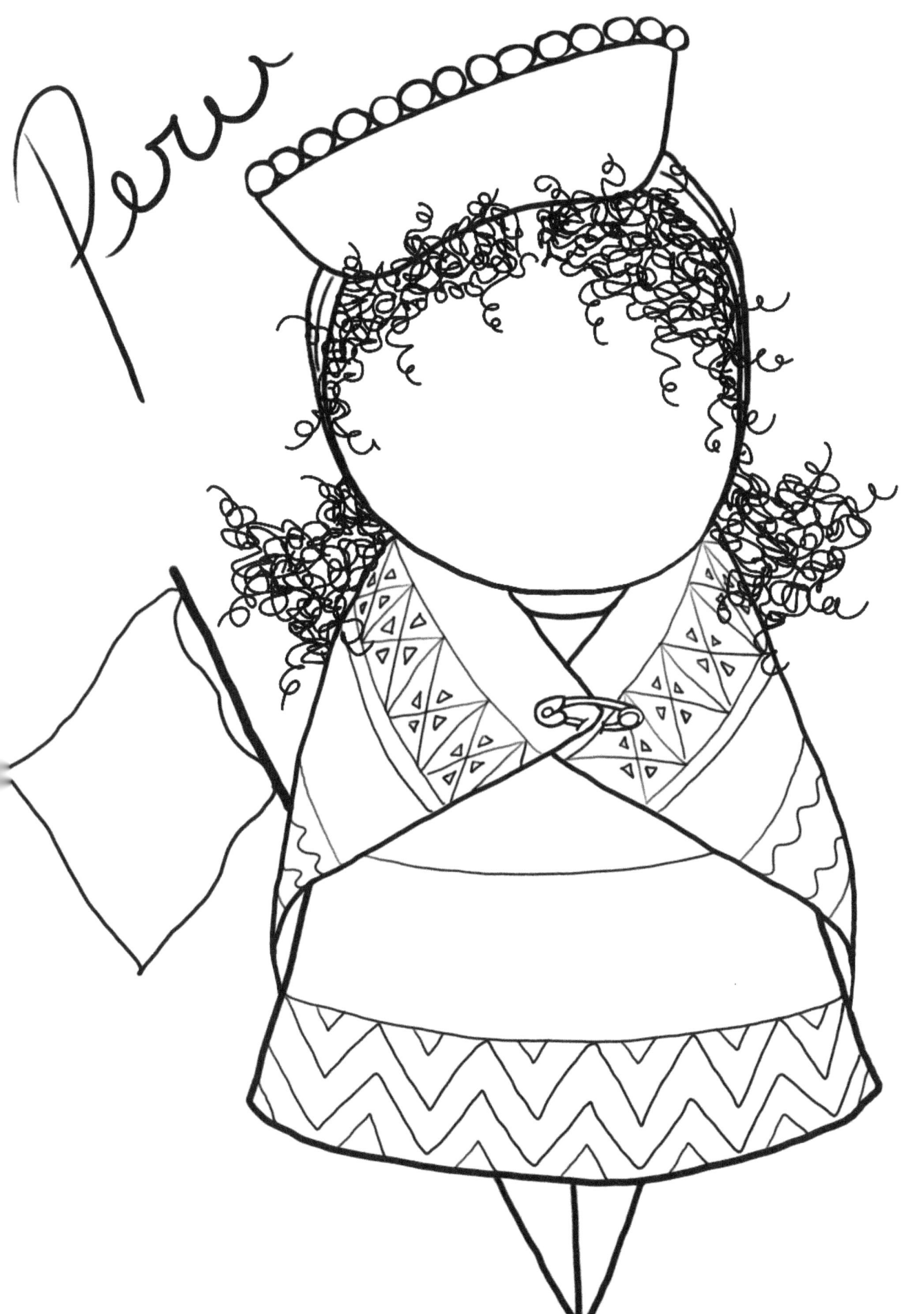

Peru

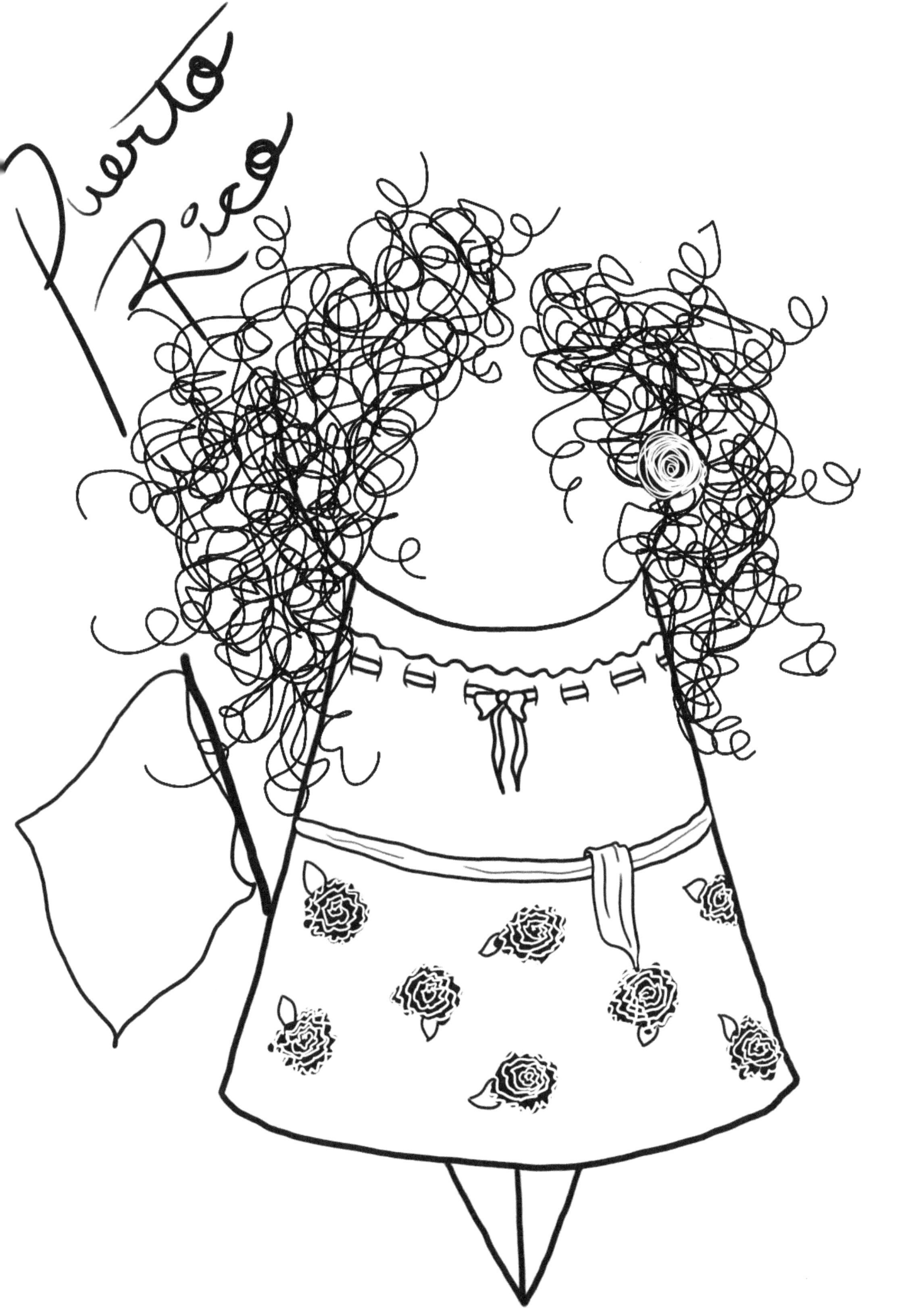

Brush

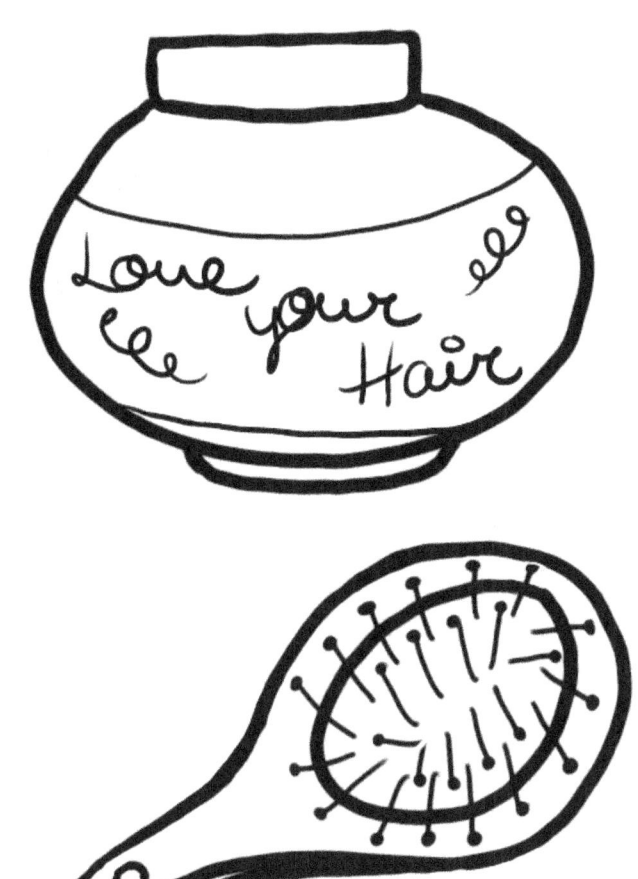

Hair
Tie

Curl
Cream

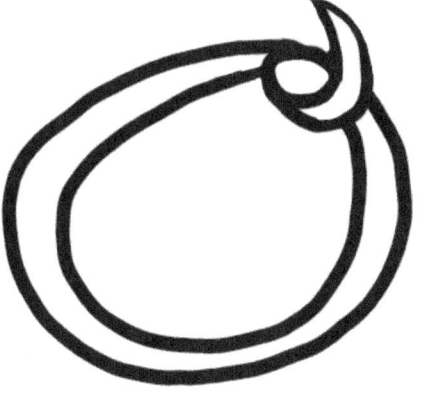

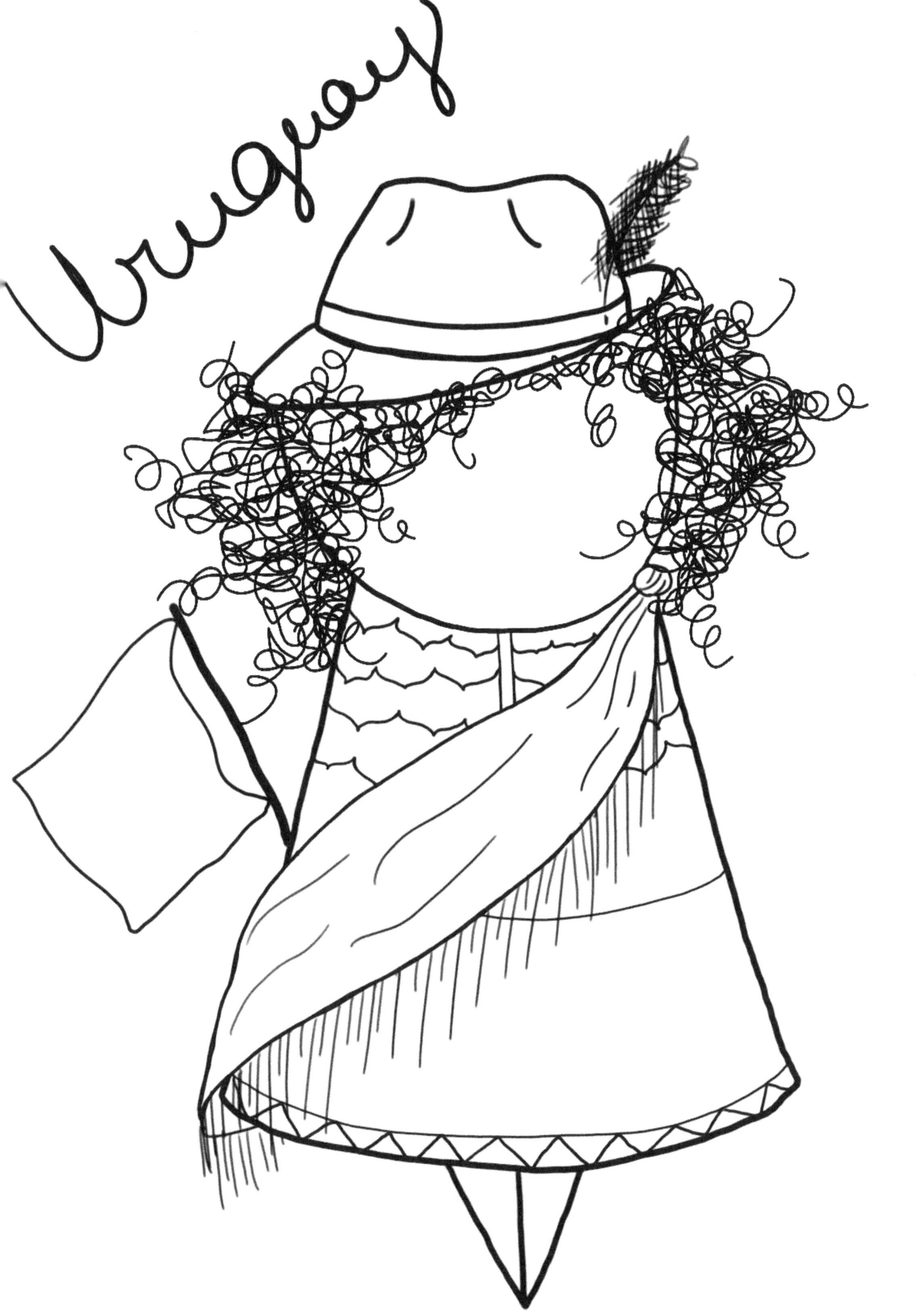

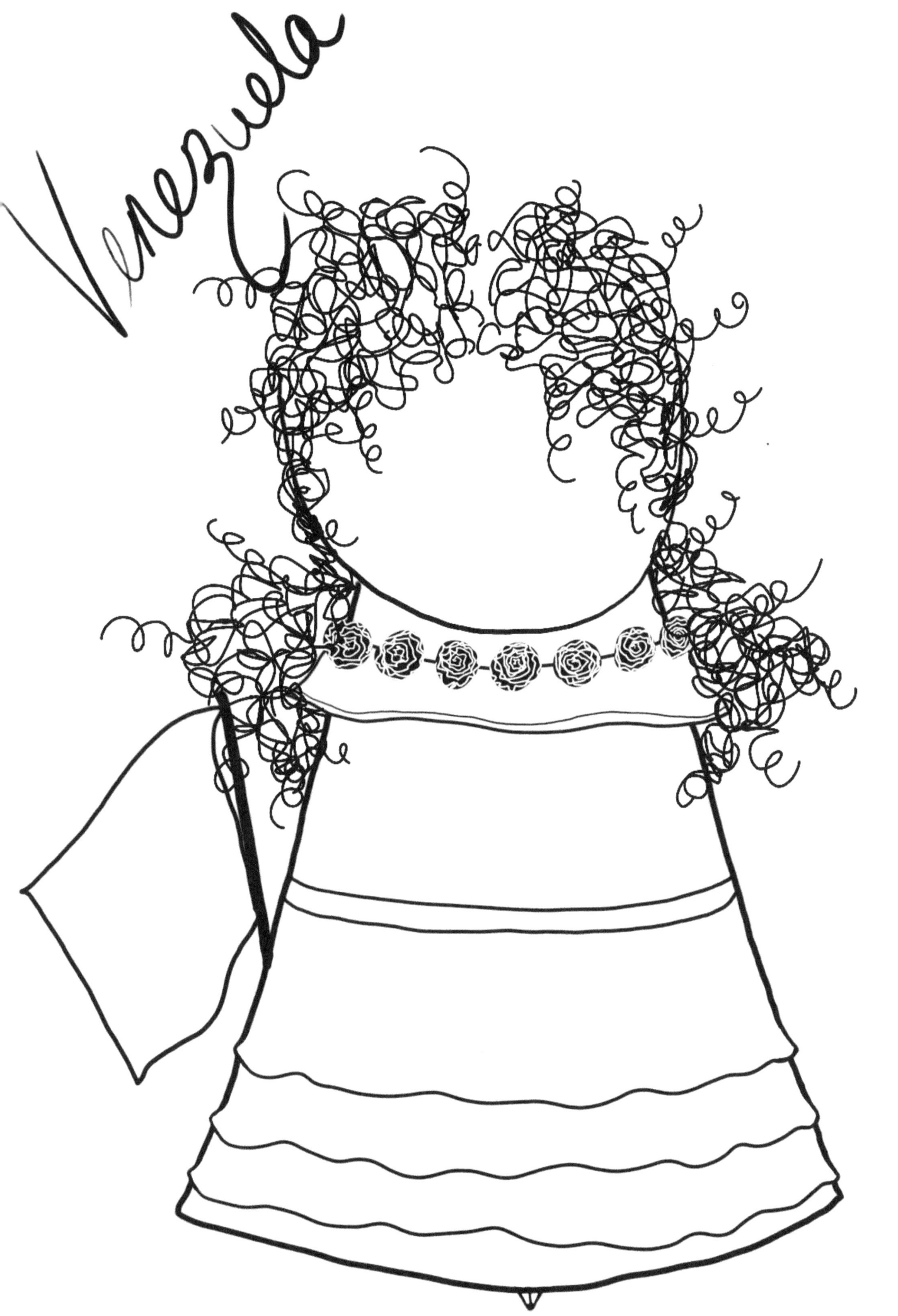